Perfection Learning®

Author

Lee Little Soldier, Ed.D.

Dr. Lee Little Soldier is a retired Texas Tech University Professor of Education. Her fields of expertise include the teaching of Language Arts, Early Childhood Education, and best practices for English Language Learners. She continues to remain active in her profession as an author, speaker, and international consultant providing in-service training to schools and universities. She is the author of two previous handwriting series published by W. S. Benson & Company.

Editorial Director: Susan C. Thies
Design Director: Randy Messer
Lead Designer: Emily J. Adickes
Illustrator: Mike Aspengren

Reviewers:

Anita Craig, Kindergarten teacher, Academic Center, Prairie Hills School District, Markham, IL

Lauren Donelson, Intervention teacher, PS7 Elementary School, St. Hope Public School District, Sacramento, CA

Janie Ephland, Literacy coach, Fort Worth Independent School District, Fort Worth, TX

Kay Iandoli, First-grade teacher, Ginnings Elementary, Denton Independent School District, Denton, TX

Amanda Jones, Third-grade teacher, Mt. Vernon Elementary School, Mt. Vernon Independent School District, Mt. Vernon, TX

Shelli Miller, First-grade teacher, Cessna Elementary School, Wichita Public School District, Wichita, KS

Sebria Mitchell, Second-grade teacher, Jackson Elementary School, Tyler Independent School District, Tyler, TX

Linnea Patrick, Third-grade teacher, Brunson Elementary School, Winston-Salem/Forsyth County School District, Winston-Salem, NC

Mariana Salazar, Second-grade bilingual teacher, Club Hill Elementary School, Garland Independent School District, Garland, TX

Cheryl Thrasher, Third-grade teacher, Everett Elementary, North Lamar Independent School District, Paris, TX

Jennifer Willden, Third-grade teacher, Hugh Gallagher Elementary School, Storey County School District, Virginia City, NV

Credits: "Silly Sally," "Slithery, Slidery, Scaly Old Snake," "The Sun Just Had a Nasty Day," and "Goose and Moose" originally published in *A Little Bit of Nonsense* by Denise Rodgers, Creative Writing Press, Inc. 2001.

7 8 9 10 11 WEBC 19 18 17 16 15
WEBC/Madison, Wisconsin, USA
06/15

ISBN-10: 0-7891-7888-5
ISBN-13: 978-0-7891-7888-6

Contents

The Mechanics of Cursive Writing

Starting with the Strokes

Using Cursive

FOCUS ON SLANT

FOCUS ON SIZE

FOCUS ON SHAPE

FOCUS ON SPACING

Time to Show Off: Pretest

Write the poem in your best cursive handwriting.

A Start

A little bit of rhythm
And a touch of funky rhyme . . .
You put them all together
And that's how I spend my time.
Tweaking all the letters
And the spaces 'tween them too,
Twirling them together
To blend up a tasty stew.
The rhythm's for my toe tap,
The idea for my mind,
The image for my inner eye,
That's like the outer kind.
I add a dash of feeling,
Just enough to touch my heart.
I'm not quite making poetry
But it is at least
A start.

by Denise Rodgers

All the Letters and Numerals

PRINTING PRACTICE

Even though you are now writing cursive, you will have times when you need to use manuscript, or printing. Write the manuscript letters below the matching cursive letters.

Aa Bb Cc Dd Ee Ff

Gg Hh Ii Jj Kk Ll

Mm Nn Oo Pp Qq Rr

Ss Tt Uu Vv Ww Xx

Yy Zz

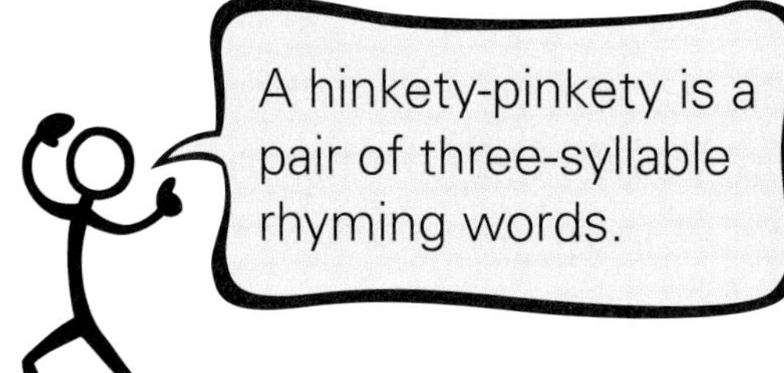

Clue: vampire's shoulder blade
Hinkety-Pinkety: dracula scapula

Use the words in the box to write the hinkety-pinkety to match each clue. Use manuscript, or printing, to write your answers. You will not use all of the words.

lottery	antelope	dinnerware	prediction
conviction	battery	umbrella	elephant
relevant	vanilla	cantaloupe	buffalo
percussion	discussion	gelatin	pottery
skeleton	bungalow	millionaire	injury

a talk about drums

wealthy person's dishes

news of an arrest

deerlike fruit

small home for a wild ox

dishes sweepstakes

bony dessert

significant mammal

flavored protection against the rain

Choose the two words that you haven't used. Write a clue for your own hinkety-pinkety.

Clue:

Hinkety-Pinkety:

Whether you are learning to kick a soccer ball, play the piano, or ride a skateboard, technique is important. The same is true with handwriting. Practicing good technique, which includes body position and how you hold the pencil or pen, will make your handwriting the best it can be.

Writing Left-Handed

If you write with your left hand:

Sit in your chair with both of your feet flat on the floor. Lean forward just a bit. Both of your arms should bend at a 90° angle to rest on your desk or table.

Slant your paper so that it is up on the left and down on the right. Hold the paper with your right hand. Use your right hand to shift your paper as you write so that you are comfortable.

Hold your pencil with your first two fingers and your thumb. Keep your first finger on top of the pencil. Don't squeeze your pencil too hard.

Writing Right-Handed

If you write with your right hand:

Sit in your chair with both of your feet flat on the floor. Lean forward just a bit. Both of your arms should bend at a 90° angle to rest on your desk or table.

Slant your paper so that it is up on the right and down on the left. Hold the paper with your left hand. Use your left hand to shift your paper as you write so that you are comfortable.

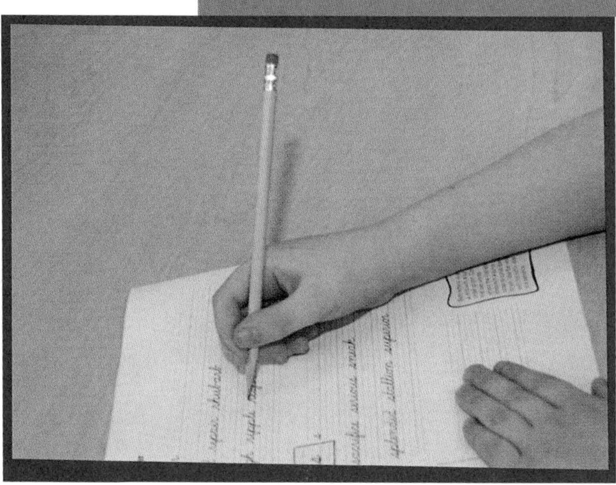

Hold your pencil with your first two fingers and your thumb. Keep your first finger on top of the pencil. Don't squeeze your pencil too hard.

Focus on Shape: Curve Under and Curve Down Strokes

Curve under is an important stroke that begins more than half of all lowercase cursive letters, as well as three capital letters. For all lowercase cursive letters, this stroke begins on the baseline. For capital cursive letters, **curve under** begins on the baseline or on the midline.

i t e u w r s l b

h k y f L S G

Practice the curve under stroke.

Curve down strokes are used in lowercase and capital cursive letters, as well as several numerals. **Curve down** strokes begin at the midline for lowercase cursive letters. **Curve down** strokes begin at the skyline for capital cursive letters and numerals.

a d o c g q C A O E D 6 8 9 0

Practice the curve down stroke.

Focus on Shape: Curve Over and Slant Down Strokes

Curve over strokes begin many capital cursive letters and only a few lowercase cursive letters. **Curve over** strokes begin at the baseline and extend to the midline for lowercase cursive letters.

n m z v x

Curve over strokes begin at the skyline for most capital cursive letters. For the last three capital cursive letters below, the curve over stroke begins on the baseline.

N M U V W X H K Y Z T F L J Q

Practice the curve over stroke.

Slant strokes begin three capital cursive letters and two numerals. Beginning slant strokes all start at the skyline. While **slant** strokes don't begin many cursive letters, they are used at least once in nearly every lowercase and capital cursive letter. This makes the slant stroke very important.

P R B / 4

Practice the slant stroke.

Focus on Slant, Size, and Spacing

Cursive letters have a forward **slant**. They *lean* forward. As you write, focus on keeping all of your letters slanting forward to the same degree. This will make the cursive letters in your words parallel. Keeping your paper slanted and shifting it as you write will help you keep your letters and words slanted.

Keep your letters slanted to the right and parallel.

Your tall letters should touch the skyline. Make your small letters half the size of your tall letters. Focus on **size** by keeping your tall letters all the same height and your small letters all the same height.

Keep your tall letters tall and your small letters small. 1 2 3

Focus on **spacing** to keep your writing legible. Make certain letters within words don't touch. The joinings should keep the letters from touching. Keep a letter-sized space between words and after the punctuation that ends a sentence.

Keep a space between words and sentences. Make sure the letters in your words don't touch.

Curve Under

i i i i i i i i i

identify ingredient intelligent

ignorant issue income

e e e e e e e e

echo enclose engineer

error evergreen exhibit

Circle the words above that begin with a curve under to curve under joining. Write a sentence below with the word that is a synonym for *mistake*.

Curve Under

u u u u u u u u

urge underground utter

unidentified uproar university

w w w w w w w

waist whistle widespread

wobble wary wilderness

The letter *w* ends with a sidestroke to join. Circle the words above that begin with a sidestroke to curve down joining. Write a sentence using two of the words above.

Curve Under

r r

reflect repair rhubarb

rough ripple responsible

s s

sacrifice serious sneak

splendid stallion superior

Both letters r and s end with a curve under to join. Circle the two words where the first letter ends with a curve under to curve down to join. Use the word with the suffix *-ible* in a sentence.

Curve Under

y y y y y y y y y

yield yonder yawn

remedy sympathy crayfish

p p p p p p p

package pheasant polite

professor puzzle pioneer

The letter *y* ends with a curve over that turns into a curve under to join. Write a sentence using the word from above that is an antonym of *rude*.

Curve Under

j j j j j j j j

jaguar jellyfish jovial

junior jewelry juvenile

t t t t t t t t

tablespoon theme thorough

tomato tread twinkle

The letter j ends with a curve over that turns into a curve under to join. Practice joining j to a, e, i, o, and u by writing the letter pairs.

Curve Under

l l l l l l l l l

lazy lettuce lieutenant

locality luggage luxury

b b b b b b b b b

banquet behavior blizzard

broccoli brilliant bushel

The letter b ends with a sidestroke to join. Circle the b joining above that requires the sidestroke to dip down a bit to create the second letter in the joining pair. Write these *be-* words to practice this joining: *beak, beard, behave, bellow, bench.*

Curve Under

h h h h h h h h

harmonize harvesting height

horrify hostile hyena

k k k k k k k k

kettle knapsack kneel

knot knuckle kingfisher

Underline the words above that begin with a silent letter. Use one of the underlined words in a sentence.

Curve Under

f f

feature fever flourish

forbidden fraction fugitive

L L

Lancing Lincoln Little Rock

Lima La Paz Libya

Circle the word above with the suffix *-en*. How did the spelling of the base word change when the suffix was added? Write your answer using your best cursive.

Curve Under

S S

Sacramento Salem Santa Fe

Springfield Sarajevo Seoul

G G

Georgia Germany Guatemala

Great Britain Greece Georgetown

Notice that S and G both end with a sidestroke right, but they are not joining letters. Underline the word above that names both a country and a state in the United States. Write a sentence using the underlined state/country.

Curve Down

a a a a a a a a a

abandon accident affection

ambition ascend assistance

o o o o o o o o o o

offensive opera organize

ornament oxygen oyster

The base word of *offensive* is *offend.* Notice how the *d* changes to an *s* when the suffix *-ive* is added. Use the word *offensive* in a sentence. Look up the meaning in a dictionary if you are not familiar with the word.

Curve Down

d d

detective discontinue dwarf

dumpling divide diamond

c c

cabinet candidate ceiling

civilization criminal cowardly

Affixes change the meanings of the root words that they are added to. The prefix *dis-* means "not" or "opposite." Circle the word that begins with the prefix *dis-*. The suffix *-ly* means "characteristic of." Underline the word with the *-ly* suffix. Use one of these words in a sentence.

Curve Down

g

gallant generation glimpse

graduate grizzly guilty

q

qualify quality quantity

quarrel quote quiver

Notice that the *q* words above all begin with *qu*. In the English language, *q* is always followed by *u*. Use the word that is an antonym for *stare* in a sentence.

Curve Down

C c

Charleston Cheyenne Columbia

Columbus Cambodia China

A a

Albany Annapolis Augusta

Austin Afghanistan Argentina

Circle the proper nouns above that have four syllables. Several of the proper nouns name capital cities in the United States. Use one in a sentence.

Curve Down

O O

Oklahoma City Olympia

Oslo Ottawa Oregon

E E

Ecuador Egypt El Salvador

England Estonia Ethiopia

D D

Denver Des Moines Dover

Denmark Dominican Republic

Curve Over

n n n n n n n n

narcissus neglect nevertheless

nightingale nucleus numerous

m m m m m m m

magnificent majesty manager

medicine microscope mourn

The word *nevertheless* is a conjunctive adverb, which is an adverb that connects and shows the relationship between two independent clauses. Use *nevertheless* in a sentence.

Curve Over

v

valuable venture veterinarian

victory volcano voyage

x

anxiety exhaust lynx

mixture relax hoax

Remember that the second stroke that finishes the x, the slant down left, is not made until you finish the word. Cursive flows because the letters are joined. Most of the time your pencil or pen should not leave the paper until you finish a word. Then you go back to cross your *t*'s, dot your *i*'s, and cross your *x*'s. Use the *x* word above that is a synonym for *trick* in a sentence.

Curve Over

Z z

zone zinc blizzard

civilization freezing horizon

N n

Nashville Namibia Nepal

Netherlands New Zealand Nigeria

Find the word above with the suffix *-ation*. Write the root word here. Use the other word above with a suffix in a sentence.

Curve Over

M m

Madison Montgomery Montpelier

Macedonia Malawi Mexico

U u

Uganda Ukraine United Kingdom

United States Uruguay Uzbekistan

The words above are all proper nouns because they name specific places. That is why they begin with capital letters. Use the proper noun above that names a country that is just south of the United States in a sentence.

Curve Over

V V

Vancouver Vatican City Venice

Venezuela Vietnam Volkswagen

W W

Wales Warsaw Washington, D.C.

Wellington Windhoek West Indies

One of the proper nouns above names a specific thing. Use that word in a sentence.

Curve Over

X X

Xanthus Xenia Xiamen

Xiang Xigu Xining

Y Y

Yemen Yukon Yangon

Yosemite Valley Yucatán Yakima

Since X is a joining letter, remember to add the second stroke (slant down to the left) after you finish writing the word. Yosemite Valley is part of Yosemite National Park in California. It has mountains, valleys, and waterfalls. Write a sentence about this valley.

Curve Over

K K K K K K K K K

Kazakhstan Kenya Kuwait

South Korea Kabul Kingstown

I I I I I I I I I

Indianapolis Iceland India

Indonesia Iran Italy

Notice that I is not a joining letter. One of the I proper nouns above is a city, while the others are all countries. Write a sentence using the I city name.

Curve Over

H H H H H H H H

Harrisburg Helena Honolulu

Haiti Honduras Hungary

Z Z Z Z Z Z Z Z

Zagreb La-Z-Boy

Zambia Zimbabwe

The Z ends with a curve over that switches to a curve under stroke to join. One of the words above is a proper noun that names a product. Use that word in a sentence.

Curve Over

J J

Jackson Jefferson City Juneau

Jamaica Japan Jordan

Q Q

Quezon City Quito Quebec

Queen Charlotte Islands Qena

The J ends with a curve over that switches to a curve under stroke to join. Q is not a joining letter. The proper nouns above all name specific places. Proper nouns can also name specific things and specific people. Several U.S. presidents had names beginning with J. Write a sentence about one of them.

Curve Over

T T T T T T T T T

Tallahassee Topeka Trenton

Taiwan Tanzania Thailand

F F F F F F F F F

Frankfurt Fiji Finland

France Freetown Fairbanks

T and F are not joining letters. Can you think of a proper noun that begins with one of the letters above and names a specific thing? Use it and write a sentence.

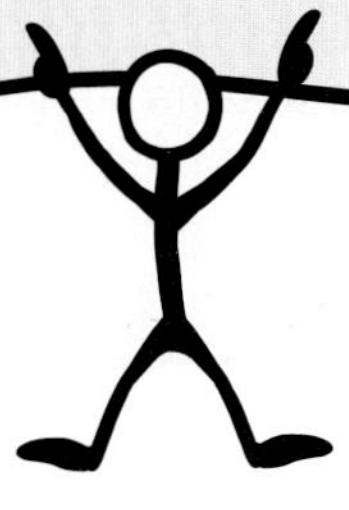

Slant Down

P P

Phoenix Pierre Providence

Pakistan Poland Portugal

R R

Raleigh Romania Russia

Rwanda Riyadh Rome

B B

Baton Rouge Bismarck Boise

Barbados Belgium Brazil

Greek and Latin Roots

PRINTING PRACTICE

Most modern English words originated in other languages. The words shown below came from the Greek and Latin languages. Use the words to answer the clues and fill in the puzzle below. Use your best printing, or manuscript handwriting.

liberty	pentagon	cinema	certain	alternate
dialogue	synonym	imitate	captain	dentist
democracy	annual	archrival	biology	

Across

3. happens every year
6. figure with five angles
9. to copy someone
11. freedom
12. main enemy
13. movie
14. word that means the same as another

Down

1. speech between two people
2. the head of a team
4. switch from one to another
5. tooth doctor
7. government by the people
8. known for sure
10. study of life

Multiple-Meaning Words

Multiple-meaning words can have many different meanings depending upon how they are used.

Read the different definitions below for the word *head.* Then write a sentence in cursive to show each definition. The first one has been done for you. Notice how the letters fit on the lines.

head *Noun* 1. the part of the body containing the brain, eyes, ears, nose, and mouth 2. the side of a coin usually thought to be the front 3. director or leader 4. a part of a machine or tool that performs the majority of the work *Verb* 5. to go in a certain direction 6. to take charge

1. The dog chewed on the head of her favorite doll.

2.

3.

4.

5.

6.

Silly Sally

When Silly Sally irons her clothes,
they come out looking awful.
She did not read the label,
and her iron was meant to waffle.

by Denise Rodgers

Analogies

An **analogy** is a logical relationship between pairs of words. Many analogies are written using antonyms and synonyms.

early : late : : wide : ________
(is to) (as) (is to)

Since *early* and *late* are antonyms, we need a word that is an antonym for *wide* to finish the analogy.

early : late : : wide : narrow

Use two words in the first box and two words in the second box to write six synonym or antonym analogies. Use each word only once. Use your best handwriting.

danger	blame	servant	grateful
exceed	master	hazard	appreciative
forgive	surpass	show	demonstrate

professor	answer	student	refuse
build	offer	clumsy	solution
destroy	construct	defeat	awkward

Are your letters slanted to the same degree?

Idioms

An **idiom** is a phrase that has a different meaning from the dictionary definitions of its individual words.

Hi Lucas. What's up?
Hi Lucas. What's new with you?

Read each sentence and study the underlined idiom. Use the context of the sentence to help you determine the meaning. Rewrite each sentence, replacing the idiom with words that show its meaning.

1. It took forever and a day to get to the front of the long line.

2. I get cold feet whenever I have to make a speech in front of people I don't know.

3. Why can't he get lost? He annoys me!

4. Maria saw a beautiful dress that really caught her eye.

continued →

Idioms continued

5. I studied my spelling words last night, so the test should be <u>a piece of cake</u>.

6. Kais <u>had us in stitches</u> when he told a funny story about his most embarrassing moment.

7. We had a <u>bird's-eye view</u> of the baseball game from the skybox.

8. We're going to be late. <u>Step on it!</u>

Check that your words all slant to the right.

Homophones

Words that sound alike but are spelled differently and have different meanings are **homophones**.

Write the homophone for each of the following words.

1. guessed
2. mist
3. fined
4. blew
5. they're
6. chews
7. haul
8. rays
9. shone
10. beet
11. road
12. weight
13. rows
14. sale
15. sun
16. herd
17. peace
18. past
19. whole
20. tide

Use a pair of the words from above. Write a sentence for each word in the pair.

Phlegm

Phlegm is the most gruesome word
that you'll find in this book.
It has a hidden silent g
that some say stands for gook.

by Denise Rodgers

Confusing Words

Read the pairs of words below and their definitions. Select one word from each pair to complete the sentences. Then write the sentences using your best handwriting.

affect (v) to change	effect (n) the result
cease (v) to stop	sieze (v) to take
council (n) a group	counsel (v) to give advice
desert (n) dry land	dessert (n) sweet treat
expect (v) to count on	suspect (v) to mistrust
loose (adj) not tight	lose (v) to not win
through (prep) in one side and out the other	thorough (adj) complete
its (pronoun) belonging to	it's (contraction) it is

1. We drove (through, thorough) the mountains in Colorado.

2. I (expect, suspect) him to win the award.

3. If we (loose, lose), we won't make it to the championship.

continued →

Confusing Words continued

4. My teacher will (cease, sieze) my phone if I use it during class.

5. For (desert, dessert) we had brownie sundaes.

6. (Its, It's) his bike that was left in the driveway.

7. The (council, counsel) voted to plan a new bike trail.

8. Not getting enough sleep did (affect, effect) his grade on the test.

Put a star next to the sentence that shows your best slant.

Time for Review: Personal Narrative

Most authors write about their own experiences. Use the lines below or another sheet of paper to write about a time when you made a choice that you later regretted.

Poetry: Free Verse

Free verse poetry is free of all the rules of poetry. It doesn't have to rhyme or have rhythm. Here is an example of free verse poetry.

Hockey

Fast break
Just me and the goalie.
I swerve right.
He leans right.
My stick goes left.
He leans left.
Wrist shot in the right corner.
Goal!

Choose something you are interested in. Write a paragraph on another sheet of paper that tells a story or expresses an opinion about your chosen subject. Make sure you have a beginning, middle, and end. Then break up the paragraph into a free verse poem. Write it on the lines below.

Make sure your capital letters are twice the size of your lowercase letters.

Alliteration

Alliteration is when beginning consonant sounds are repeated in neighboring words. Read the poem below and enjoy the alliteration.

Slithery, Slidery, Scaly Old Snake

Slithery, slidery, scaly old snake,
Surely your body must be a mistake.
Your eyes, mouth, and tongue wisely stay on your head.
It seems that your body is all tail instead.
You gobble your dinner, you swallow it whole—
A mouse or a frog or a turtle or mole.
Ugh!
Why don't you eat ice cream or chocolatey cake!
Oh slithery, slidery, scaly old snake.

by Denise Rodgers

Think of words to fill in the blanks below to create alliteration. Then write the sentences.

1. *Allison* ______ *ate* _____ *and anchovies.*

2. _______ *Jones juggled* __________, *jiggly* __________.

continued →

Alliteration continued

3. Shondra __________ shivered in a __________ shirt.

4. Gretchen __________ gobbled a __________ of green __________.

5. Norbert __________ never __________ new __________.

Now write a sentence of your own with alliteration.

Personification

Personification is a figure of speech that gives human qualities to objects, ideas, and animals. In the poem below, the Sun is being personified, or given human qualities.

The Sun Just Had a Nasty Day

The Sun just had a nasty day,
refused to smile or shine.
It stayed behind the dark gray clouds,
a mottled, grim design.
But shortly after dinnertime
one ray poked through the gray,
a spark of golden yellow warmth
reminding us of day.

If you want to please us, Sun,
(don't take this as a warning)
if you're going to pierce the clouds,
please do it in the morning.

by Denise Rodgers

Read the sentences below. Circle the idea, object, or animal being personified. Underline the personification. Then write the sentence using your best handwriting.

1. The darkness wrapped its arms around the lonely children.

2. The fireflies played tag in the night air.

continued ➔

Personification continued

3. My homework cried out for me to finish it before bedtime.

4. The large bush refused to budge when Dad tried to dig it up.

5. As I jumped across the stream, a vine grabbed my foot.

Now write your own personification sentence about the moon.

Look at the word *vine* in sentence 5. Are all the letters the same height?

Focus on Size

Hyperbole

Hyperbole is a figure of speech that shows exaggeration and is not meant to be taken seriously. Read the following example.

> The north wind blew so hard that the Sun felt cold.

Read the paragraphs below. Underline each example of hyperbole. Then rewrite the paragraphs using your best handwriting. Concentrate on the slant and size of your letters.

Maria took her place at the podium. She was so scared she nearly passed out. Her teacher said she was the best speller in the world, but she got nervous in front of an audience. Her legs were trembling so much that the whole stage shook.

"Your word is buoyancy," said the announcer.

Why did I have to get the only word I don't know how to spell? she thought. Her heart was pounding so loud that she knew everyone could hear it.

Circle a word in your paragraphs that shows tall, small, and below-the-line letters. Are your letters sized properly?

Drama PRINTING PRACTICE

Drama is a play to be read or performed on a stage. Readers learn the story by understanding what the characters say to one another. The actual words the characters say is called *dialogue*. Stage directions tell what the characters do.

stage directions

dialogue

character

KATIA: *(in a voice filled with terror)* Mom! Dad!

DAD: *(entering with MOM)* What is it, Kat?

KATIA: They said on TV that Lela Ramos is missing.

Rewrite the following as a play. Use manuscript writing, or printing. Don't forget stage directions.

"Please come in here," Dad called from the kitchen.

Gabriela sauntered into the kitchen. "What's up?" she asked.

"I'll tell you what's up," Dad said as he pointed to the counters.

"Oops," said Gabriela, as she looked at her toes. "Guess I forgot to clean up after I made nachos."

DAD:

GABRIELA:

DAD:

GABRIELA:

When you use manuscript writing, you have a midline to guide the size of your small letters. Do your small letters touch the midline. Do your tall letters touch the skyline?

Summarizing

A **summary** is a shortened version of a text containing only the key points, or important facts. To summarize a passage or selection, retell the main idea and important details in your own words.

Read the paragraphs. Then summarize below.

The Eiffel Tower is a popular sight in Paris, France, with an interesting history. It is 300 meters tall and weighs 7,000 tons. Gustave Eiffel was the tower's designer. It was built for the 1889 International Exhibition of Paris. Over the years, the Eiffel Tower has been the site of some very interesting scenes.

In 1954, a mountaineer climbed up the side of the tower. That sight must have startled the people nearby. In 1984, two Englishmen parachuted off the tower. I'd like to have seen that. And a journalist rode a bicycle down from the first level in 1923. He probably had a very bumpy ride.

When it was first built, many people in Paris hated the tower. They thought it was ugly. The tower was almost torn down in 1909. But today, it is as beloved a structure in Paris as it has become to the rest of the world.

Main Idea of the Passage

continued →

Summarizing continued

1st Supporting Fact

2nd Supporting Fact

3rd Supporting Fact

Fact and Opinion

A **fact** is a true statement that can be proven. An **opinion** is a statement that tells what someone feels or believes, which may vary from person to person and cannot be proven.

Read the paragraphs below. Underline the opinion sentences. Then write them on the lines below.

Kangaroos are native to Australia. I love Australia. It is a beautiful place.

Kangaroos are the only large mammals that can hop. Australia can get very hot in the daytime, so kangaroos rest during the hottest part of the day. To help keep cool, they pant; lie in holes in shady, sandy areas; and lick their arms. I'd hate to have to lick my arms to stay cool! They become active and eat in the evening or at night. Meals for kangaroos consist of grasses, leaves, and the shoots of small trees.

Kangaroos live in groups called mobs. A female kangaroo is called a doe. The male is called a buck. Babies are called joeys. When joeys are born, I think they look very strange.

Do your below-the-line letters descend below the baseline without touching the tall letters below?

Text Structures: Compare and Contrast

To **compare** means to identify how things are alike. To **contrast** means to identify how things are different.

Read the paragraphs below. Write the sentences that compare, or tell what is true of both, in the first section. Write the sentences that contrast, or talk about differences between the two, in the second section.

Roller skates and the skateboard were two favorite toys of the twentieth century. Both toys have wheels. Roller skates are a pair of boots or soles with wheels attached. A skateboard is a small board with wheels on the bottom. Both toys are still popular today.

In 1760 in Belgium, Joseph Merlin invented the first roller skates. He wore a pair of skates to a party in London. Merlin couldn't skate very well and crashed into a mirror! He didn't skate much after that.

No one knows who invented the skateboard. In the 1950s surfing was big in California. It was during this time that someone decided to "surf" the streets. A smaller version of a surfboard was then placed on wheels. Skateboard mania took off.

Compare

Contrast

Text Structures: Procedural Text

PRINTING PRACTICE

Procedural text tells step-by-step how to do something. Recipes and driving directions are examples of procedural text.

The sentences below are driving directions. They are out of order. Read them and rewrite them in order below. Use manuscript writing, or printing.

Turn left from NW 142nd Street onto SE University Avenue.
101 Jordan Creek Parkway, or Jordan Creek Town Center, is on the right.
Continue on NW 142nd Street for 1 mile.
Continue on Jordan Creek Parkway for .02 mile.
Begin at 2680 Berkshire Parkway.
Turn right from Hickman Road/HWY 6 onto NW 142nd Street.
Turn right from SE University Avenue onto Jordan Creek Parkway.
Turn left from Berkshire Parkway onto Hickman Road/HWY 6.

Check the size of your letters. Use the guidelines.

Graphs

A line **graph** shows changes over time.

Study the graph below. Then write five sentences that explain the graph.

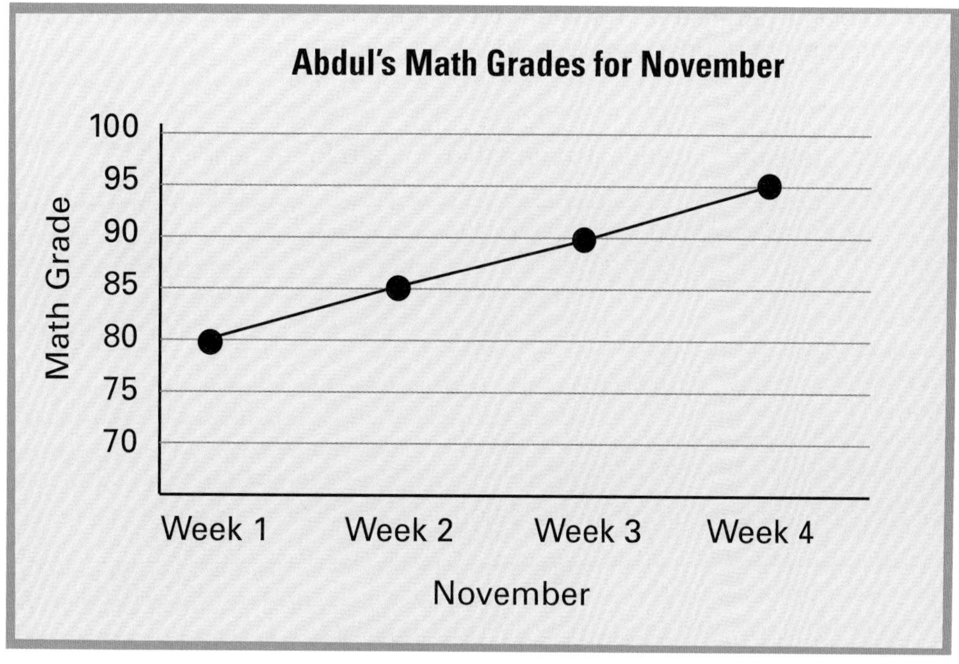

Time for Review: Persuasive Writing

Persuasive writing is about taking a position for or against something and convincing your audience to agree with you.

Use the form below to plan a persuasive argument for or against having pop machines in schools. Your audience is the principal of your school. Use your best handwriting.

Opening statement. State the question and whether you are for or against it.

First argument or reason in support of your position.

Second argument or reason in support of your position.

Third argument or reason in support of your position.

continued ➜

Time for Review: Persuasive Writing continued

Conclusion. Restate the question and your position. Then tell your reader what to do.

Plot PRINTING PRACTICE

A **plot** is what happens in a story. **Plot** is a series of events surrounding a problem that needs to be solved.

Read the following story. Then answer the questions about the plot. Use manuscript writing, or printing.

The Powerful Fly

Once there was a river in a valley. It was the most beautiful river in the world. Fish, beavers, and muskrats lived peacefully in and near its crystal waters.

One day a moose came into the valley. It took a sip of the crystal water. Delighted, it guzzled down more and more. The river grew smaller and smaller. That night the fish, beavers, and muskrats met together. None could think of a plan to save their beautiful river. A fly overheard their talk and said he would take care of the problem.

That thirsty moose arrived again the next morning. The fly landed on its back and bit the moose. The moose jumped in anger. The fly kept biting the moose until it was wild with anger. The moose ran away and never returned to the happy little valley.

1. What is the setting of the story?

2. What is the first event in the story?

3. What is the problem in the story?

4. What is the solution in the story?

Point of View

Point of view describes who is telling a story. When the narrator is a character in the story, the story is written in first-person point of view.

I walked across the street to the drugstore.

When the narrator is an outside observer and tells about other characters, the story is written in third-person point of view.

Eduardo walked across the street to the drugstore.

The following paragraph is written in first-person point of view. The narrator is the main character in the story. Assign the narrator a name and rewrite the paragraph in third-person point of view.

I just don't get it. My dad signed us up for mountain-climbing lessons—like I have the time during school. All he has to do is go to work, but I have to go to school and do homework. My friend Darren and his dad took scuba-diving lessons. Darren flunked a test because he didn't have time to study. Summertime would be okay, but right now, I have a report to write.

In the paragraph that is written for you, circle the capital letters that do not join. Then check to make sure they are not joined in the paragraph you wrote.

Focus on Shape

Similes

A **simile** is figurative language that compares two unlike things using the words *like* or *as*.

Numbers swam in my head like a school of fish.

Rewrite each sentence below using the actual meaning rather than the simile.

1. All the neighborhood dogs barked like cannons firing in loud explosions.

2. As we walked in the woods, the leaves were like crunchy cornflakes beneath our feet.

3. My thoughts were heavy as bricks because I dreaded sharing the bad news.

4. Sunshine was like a warm bath on my face, telling me that spring had finally arrived.

continued →

Similes continued

5. My teacher is like a walking encyclopedia when he talks about the American Revolution.

6. The sea is like a road for ships.

7. His dirty clothing looked like a mountain after vacation.

8. The janitor moved through the rooms like a tornado as he cleaned after school.

Does your cursive writing flow? Are your joinings smooth?

Metaphors

A **metaphor** is figurative language that compares two unlike things but does not use the words *like* or *as*.

That running back is a <u>bull in a china shop</u> when he runs down the field.

metaphor

Rewrite the following paragraph below. Replace the underlined phrases with new metaphors.

With two seconds left in the game, DeWayne took his place at the free throw line. His heart was <u>a hammer pounding in his chest</u>, but he had inner confidence. The old gymnasium was <u>a sweatbox</u>, and DeWayne tried to dry his hands on his shorts before he took the ball from the referee. His first shot was <u>a high rainbow</u> that hung on the rim for a second and then dropped through. The crowd's roar was <u>a swelling ocean wave</u>. Relieved at having tied the game, DeWayne calmly sank the second free throw as well. He was <u>a door slamming</u> the other team's hopes of a championship!

In order for your handwriting to be legible, your letters must have good shape. Check to make sure your *e*'s and *l*'s are open so they aren't confused with other letters.

Quotation Marks

A direct quotation is the exact words of a person. Use **quotation marks** before and after a direct quotation.

> Pedro said, "The baseball game will have to be cancelled."
>
> The quotation marks come before and after the exact words spoken.

Read the sentences below. Add quotation marks before and after the exact words spoken. Then rewrite the sentences correctly.

1. It's time for you to leave, Mrs. O'Reilly told us.

2. The author wrote, I can't seem to shake my writer's block.

3. Ester explained, That's what happens when you don't get enough sleep.

4. Stop right where you are! the policeman told the suspect.

continued →

Quotation Marks continued

5. The actor yelled, Let's get out of here!

6. Shielding her eyes from the sun, Yolanda said, It's going to be a hot day.

7. Do you know Pia's phone number? Juan asked me.

Write your own sentence with a direct quotation.

Time for Review: Friendly Letters

Friendly letters are written to a friend or family member. Friendly letters should include the date, the salutation (greeting), body, closing, and signature.

Use the form below to write a friendly letter to a friend or family member. Use your best handwriting.

Irregular Verbs

Irregular verbs don't form past tense versions by adding *-ed* or *-d.*

	present tense	past tense
Regular Verb:	walk	walked
Irregular Verb:	run	ran

Underline the incorrect irregular verb in each sentence below. Correct the verb and rewrite the sentence. Make sure you leave space between each word in the sentence.

1. Maraya bringed her new iPod to school.

2. He catched the flu from his best friend.

3. The family always sitted down to dinner together.

4. We couldn't believe our team winned the championship.

5. Darius runned to catch the bus.

continued →

word wor

Irregular Verbs continued

6. No one ever thinked he'd get the award.

7. The pitcher throwed the ball right over the plate. Strike!

8. Lateia knowed everybody at the party.

word wor

Collective Nouns

Collective nouns name groups of things composed of individual members.

If the group is acting together, use a singular verb.

acting as one
The class takes time to read silently after recess.
singular verb

If each member of the group is acting as an individual, use a plural verb.

plural verb
The class bring their own books for silent reading.
acting as individuals plural pronoun

Use the collective nouns below in two sentences. Write one sentence with a singular verb where the group is acting as one. Then write a second sentence with a plural verb where each member is acting as an individual. Use your best handwriting.

team

audience

family

word wor

Noncount Nouns

Noncount nouns do not have a singular and plural form. A noncount noun takes a singular verb. Do not use *a* or *an* in front of a noncount noun.

Rice is one of my favorite foods.
(is — singular verb; Rice — noncount noun)

Choose four noncount nouns from those listed below. Use each in a sentence.

grass	fruit	hair	fog
sand	soap	paint	salt

1.

2.

3.

4.

Goose and Moose

It's hard to tell just what a goose
Will have in common with a moose.
Or better yet, just what three geese
Will have in common with three meese.
(Is that the plural for a mouse?
Is grice the plural for three grouse?)
I'll say this once. I'll say this thrice.
The plural for a moose is mice,
Or plural for three mice is meeses.
I think that I may fall to pieces.
I feel my dizzy states increase
about the mice, the grice, and geese.

by Denise Rodgers

word wor

Adjectives: Comparative and Superlative

Comparative adjectives compare two things. Add *-er* to form comparative adjectives.

> Delon is taller than his twin Keenan.
> the two boys are being compared

Superlative adjectives compare three or more things. Add *-est* to form superlative adjectives.

> Delon is the tallest boy in his class.
> three or more boys

Write the comparative and superlative forms of the adjectives below.

1. large
2. long
3. cold
4. quiet
5. great
6. smart
7. hungry
8. big
9. strong
10. easy

Use one of the comparative adjectives and write a sentence below.

Predicate Adjectives

A **predicate adjective** is an adjective that follows a linking verb and modifies, or describes, the subject.

> linking verb
> The spider monkey <u>is</u> intelligent.
> subject predicate adjective

Read the sentences below. Underline the linking verb. Draw an arrow from the subject to the predicate adjective that modifies it. Then rewrite the sentences using your best handwriting. Remember to space your words so that they can be easily read.

1. The cafeteria can be noisy.

2. That test seemed hard.

3. The wind feels colder today.

4. My sister is famous.

5. The pizza tasted delicious.

6. He felt sad when he heard the news.

7. My homework is finished.

Adverbs

An **adverb** is a word that modifies, or describes, a verb, an adjective, or an adverb. Many adverbs end in *-ly*. Adverbs usually explain *How? When? Where?*

He ran quickly when his name was called.
adverb
The adverb *quickly* tells how he ran.

Underline the adverb in each sentence below. Draw an arrow from the adverb to the word it modifies, or describes. Then rewrite the sentence.

1. Kangaroos rarely eat insects.

2. The thunder was extremely loud.

3. Two women amazingly survived the accident.

4. The boat's engine abruptly stopped in the middle of the lake.

5. Eduardo angrily took the toy from his sister.

continued ➜

Adverbs continued

6. Aman makes his bed neatly before he goes downstairs.

7. Lavinia frequently shops with her mom.

8. The firefighters arrived immediately.

Check your spacing. Is it clear where one word ends and the other begins?

word wor

Prepositions

A **preposition** is a word that shows the relationship between a noun or a pronoun and another word in the sentence.

A bird sat on the roof.
preposition
The preposition shows location.

Choose a preposition from the box to complete the sentences below. You will use some of the prepositions more than once. Then rewrite the sentences.

of	within	in	for
on	at	with	to

1. A museum __________ Boston once had a wonderful idea.

2. It sold land __________ the surface __________ the moon.

3. All __________ the lots had a good view __________ Earth.

4. The prices started __________ $25.

continued →

Prepositions continued

5. All owners received deeds ____________ their moon property.

6. These unofficial deeds came ____________ certain rights.

7. ____________ these rights, owners made a promise.

8. They had to respect any moon creatures ____________ their property.

Check your letter spacing. If your letters are slanted properly, none of them should touch.

Prepositional Phrases

Prepositions and **prepositional phrases** convey location, time, direction, or provide details in a sentence.

Read the sentences below. Underline the prepositional phrase. Write *location, time, direction,* or *details* on the blank. Then rewrite the sentence.

1. We could see across the bay. ____________________

2. Let's run around the track. ____________________

3. Monkeys live in almost every tropical climate. ____________________

4. Before Friday I didn't have any tests. ____________________

5. With the extra help, we should finish soon. ____________________

6. Close the window during the storm. ____________________

continued →

word wor

Prepositional Phrases continued

7. The building at the intersection is the school. ____________________

8. During intermission no one left. ____________________

9. They will take us with them. ____________________

10. They used the money for additional exhibits and programs.

____

word wor

Reflexive Pronouns

The suffix *-self* or *-selves* can be added to some personal pronouns to form **reflexive pronouns**.

reflexive pronoun

Rashan helped himself to more pie.

The reflexive pronoun *himself* refers to Rashan.

Read the sentences below. Underline the reflexive pronoun and draw an arrow to the noun or pronoun it refers to. Then rewrite the sentence using your best handwriting.

1. The twins treated themselves to a banana split after the volleyball game.

2. The cat was sunning itself underneath the window.

3. Flor cried herself to sleep.

4. I was beside myself with laughter.

continued ➜

word wor

Reflexive Pronouns continued

5. She saw herself reflected in the store window.

6. We let ourselves into the house for the surprise party.

7. The dancers watched themselves in the mirror as they practiced.

8. Marc tied his shoelaces himself.

Indefinite Pronouns

Indefinite pronouns are words that replace nouns without specifying which noun they replace. Singular indefinite pronouns take singular verbs. Plural indefinite pronouns take plural verbs.

Common Indefinite Pronouns	
Singular	anybody, anyone, anything, each, either, everybody, everyone, neither, nobody, no one, some, someone
Plural	all, both, few, many, others, several

Each of the sentences below has an indefinite pronoun. Underline the indefinite pronoun. Read and decide whether the pronoun takes a singular verb or plural verb. Then rewrite the sentence.

1. Someone in this classroom (is, are) not telling the truth.

2. As for the apples on the tree in the backyard, few (is, are) ripe enough to pick.

3. Many (take, takes) this exact route to work each day.

4. One of Sally's uncles (was, were) involved in the accident.

continued ➜

Indefinite Pronouns continued

5. Several of her summer vacations (has, have) been to Colorado.

6. Nobody (was, were) signing up for Glee Club.

7. One of the students in this room (is, are) the winner.

8. Each of the band members (is, are) going to Florida.

9. Yes, both of you (needs, need) new shoes.

10. Either Helena or Missoula (is, are) the capital of Montana.

Correlative Conjunctions

Conjunctions are connective words, and **correlative conjunctions** are pairs of connecting words used together in different parts of a sentence.

Correlative Conjunctions		
both/and	either/or	neither/nor

Read the sentences and underline the pairs of correlative conjunctions. Then rewrite the sentences.

1. We can get the book either at the bookstore or at the library.

2. The answer is neither A nor B.

3. Both my mother and my father graduated from the University of Wisconsin.

4. We can either go boating or go swimming.

5. Choosing a career is both challenging and exciting.

Use one of the correlative conjunction pairs in a sentence of your own.

word wor

Transition Words

Transitions are words and phrases that show the passing of time.

Transition Words that Show Time Order		
before	finally	after
first	next	later
when	then	one day

Read the paragraph below. Find and underline the transition words. Then rewrite the paragraph below, remembering to space your words.

I had a big surprise the first time I went to the dentist. One day when I was five, my mother told me I had to go to the dentist. I was so nervous that I tried hiding in the basement. My mother finally found me, though, and off we went to the dentist. When I sat down in Dr. Pearlman's chair, I really tensed up. To my surprise, though, she didn't even examine the inside of my mouth. All she did that day was talk to me and take X-rays. None of my fears came to pass.

Complete Subjects and Predicates

A **complete subject** includes all the words used to identify the person, place, thing, or idea that the sentence is about. A **complete predicate** includes all the words that tell what the subject is doing or that tell something about the subject.

Most Bengal tigers live in India.
Most Bengal tigers — complete subject; live in India. — complete predicate

Read the sentences below. Underline the complete subject and circle the complete predicate. Then rewrite the sentences using your best handwriting.

1. Most plants grow from seeds.

2. The banana plant has no seeds.

3. Rows of flowers grow under the leaves.

4. A hand of bananas grows from each row.

continued →

word wor

Complete Subjects and Predicates
continued

5. About ten hands grow on each plant.

6. Its pollen grains are like yellow dust.

7. Currents of air carry pollen from one flower to another.

8. Strong winds may blow pollen grains 60 miles from their plant.

9. More than 200 grains could fit on the head of a pin.

10. A single birch tree can produce five billion grains.

word wor

Subject/Verb Agreement

When the parts of a **compound subject** are joined by *and*, use a plural verb.

> Enrica <u>and</u> Rita help the teacher one day a week after school.
> ↑ plural verb

When the parts of a **compound subject** are joined by *or*, *either/or*, or *neither/nor*, use a singular verb.

> <u>Either</u> Enrica <u>or</u> Rita helps the teacher one day a week after school.
> ↑ singular verb

Read the sentences below. Underline the correct verb choice. Then rewrite the sentence.

1. Basketball and handball (is, are) played on hard courts.

2. Maples and oaks (drops, drop) their leaves in the fall.

3. Neither the umbrella nor the tree (protects, protect) us from the sun.

4. Either the mayor or his assistant (runs, run) the meetings.

continued →

word wor

Subject/Verb Agreement continued

5. Gold and silver (is, are) valuable metals.

6. Copper or platinum (is, are) added to gold.

7. Gold and other precious metals (was, were) mined by ancient peoples.

8. Neither gold nor silver jewelry (is, are) hard enough without adding copper or platinum.

word wor

Active and Passive Voice

The **active voice** indicates that the subject is performing the action.

> My father drove me to Shontelle's house.
> subject — Father is doing the driving.

The **passive voice** indicates that the action of the verb is being performed upon the subject.

> I was driven to Shontelle's house by my father.
> subject — The subject is not performing the action.

Read the sentences below. Underline the verb. Decide whether the verb is in the active voice or passive voice. Then rewrite the sentence.

1. *The judge gives the signal.* active or passive

2. *The tree bark was eaten by white-tailed deer.* active or passive

3. *Dad prepared a special birthday dinner.* active or passive

4. *Dan was promised a place on the first team.* active or passive

5. *Sonja will buy the cake and decorate it.* active or passive

Check your word spacing.

Time for Review: Sensory Details

Writers use **sensory details** to make their stories come alive for readers. These are details that involve sight, touch, sound, smell, or taste.

Study the illustration to the right. Then write a sentence about the illustration for each of the senses listed.

Sight

Sound

Smell

Taste

Touch

Time to Show Off: Posttest

This is the poem you wrote at the beginning of this book. Write the poem again in your best cursive handwriting. Compare it to the first time you wrote it and celebrate how much you've learned!

A Start

A little bit of rhythm
And a touch of funky rhyme . . .
You put them all together
And that's how I spend my time.
Tweaking all the letters
And the spaces 'tween them too,
Twirling them together
To blend up a tasty stew.
The rhythm's for my toe tap,
The idea for my mind,
The image for my inner eye,
That's like the outer kind.
I add a dash of feeling,
Just enough to touch my heart.
I'm not quite making poetry
But it is at least
A start.

by Denise Rodgers